Endorsements: 'You live forever'

Gladys: Thank you for sharing Chapter I & II with me, I will be looking forward to reading another chapter one of these days. Bob Durst, MD, Topeka Ks

Gladys: Thank you for writing "you live forever". It was wonderful, and I have shared it several times. Clara George, Missouri

Gladys: Never in my wildest dreams would I ever expect some one I know would have an experience like you and survive to write this unique book, it was wonderful. Thank you. Twila & Bob Stapel, Kansas

Gladys: This book was wonderful and beautiful, I find it easy to believe. I love how you have written it as well. I take comfort in that, and in what you have to say to me as well. My mother saw an Angel when she died. Iris Wylie, Missouri

Gladys: I read your book and found it beautiful, can I send it to other people. Karen Thompson, Arizona

Gladys: Erma and I really enjoyed your book, we thought it was wonderful. We are grateful you came back to share it with us.
Your brother John Thompson, Arizona

Gladys: We so enjoyed your book, Chapter 2, looking forward for more chapters. I truly believe you saw what you saw, you were blessed. All my church friends are looking forward to your book. Omega Cole, Illinois

Gladys: That was beautiful and has just increased my belief, thanks for sharing. Nadeane Wood, Kansas

Gladys: I really enjoyed your book. It gave me peace of mind. I think God is telling us something. Beth Uber, Illinois

Gladys: Thanks for sharing your story. I believe it. There is no doubt that God has great things waiting for us. Keep writing, George Ogan, Kansas

"You live forever"

Gladys L. Hargis

WestBow
PRESS
A DIVISION OF THOMAS NELSON

WestBow Press books may be ordered through booksellers or by contacting:

WestBow Press
A Division of Thomas Nelson
1663 Liberty Drive
Bloomington, IN 47403
www.westbowpress.com
1-(866) 928-1240

Because of the dynamic nature of the Internet, any Web addresses or links contained in this book may have changed since publication and may no longer be valid. The views expressed in this work are solely those of the author and do not necessarily reflect the views of the publisher, and the publisher hereby disclaims any responsibility for them.

Any people depicted in stock imagery provided by Thinkstock are models, and such images are being used for illustrative purposes only.

Certain stock imagery © Thinkstock.

ISBN: 978-1-4497-0923-5 (sc)
ISBN: 978-1-4497-0924-2 (dj)
ISBN: 978-1-4497-0922-8 (e)

Library of Congress Control Number: 2010941414

Printed in the United States of America

WestBow Press rev. date: 12/13/2010

In memory of my childhood friend:

Beth Jeffries Uber

Contents

This information came from Gladys Hargis of Topeka, Kansas. It is my true story about having a near death experience in August 2006, I can only tell you what I saw, but there are no words to describe it all. It was beautiful and beyond description. It has changed my life forever, and I witness about it every chance I get.

There are Angels present, long before your soul leaves your body, and when your body is sinking low they will make their presence known.

This book will help to ease the pain and separation of our family and friends that we will all have to endure someday.

God and his Angels will be with you always. So have no fear.

I hope you will all enjoy this book as much as I have in writing it.

ACKNOWLEDGMENT:

I wrote this book because I wanted to tell everyone what I saw beyond this world.

I knew for a fact that it was real, because usually when you just dream, you wake up, and cannot remember all of the details, just sketches. This is imprinted in my memory, and will be there for my life time.

I want to thank my niece Ruth Ann Maus, who had medical knowledge, to help encourage the Doctors at Stormont Vail Hospital in Topeka Kansas, to try everything they could do to help save my life, because no one knew what was wrong with me. They didn't need much encouragement, but I understood later, at times they almost gave up hope. I want to thank the Topeka Fire Department, who arrived first, and tried to stabilize me. I want to thank the American Medical Response team, who took over and worked on me to keep me breathing.

My thanks go out to Dr. Kingfisher, and his assistants in the emergency room, who brought me back to life, not just once but twice. I was put on life support until they could decide what was wrong with me.

When I once asked if I was going to live, I heard a shout, "yes you are", which was encouraging.

My special thanks go out to: Dr. Arfaei, Dr. Malik, Dr. Graham, Dr. Gandhi, Dr. Patel, Dr. Leeds, Dr. Tan, and Dr. McKee, a hospital consultant. Dr. Rankin, and all the nurses in the ICU unit who watched over me every minute of the eight days I was in intensive care.

I want to especially thank Rose Marie Steenhoven, Rene, & Jeanette nurses on the sixth floor who took care of me on my long road back. I want to also thank the angels who watched over me and gave me courage too want to live. The other world is so peaceful and I can hardly wait to go again, but I had a job to do, and with everyone's encouragement I knew I would return to this world.

A special thanks to my sister Joy Law, who came to my bedside and kept me lucid asking me questions like, what I saw in Heaven. Do the angels have wings? Tell me everything you have seen. I was so excited everyday she came that I had to tell someone who would listen to my stories. She told me later that I had awakened once singing "Bringing in the Sheaves". The staff in ICU and my sister said I sang every verse. I didn't think I even knew every verse. I just was bubbling over with excitement, while awake. I made several trips to Heaven.

I want to again give a special thanks again to Dr. Arfaei, my lung doctor, who believed in me, and he acknowledge that I indeed must have seen something wonderful, when I had a close brush with death.

I want to thank Heidi Kuglin, for her help and support.

I want to thank Pastor Bob Hattle, a Presbyterian minister, who on Valentine's day 2010, used part of my book with his sermon.

And finally I want to give a special thanks to my husband who was with me continually through this ordeal. He was, as I was, in awe of what I had seen of my journey into the other world. He too was given a great gift, to witness an angel, who was still watching over me in my room. It made a believer out of him, and he thanks God everyday for this honor.

I hope this book brings you, my readers, peace, and the acknowledgement that LOVE conquers all, and that GOD is great.

SECTION I

CHAPTER I

"The Doorway to Heaven"

One Friday afternoon, as we sat on the porch enjoying Indian summer, my husband Warren and I were talking about a couple who had died within days of each other. Warren and I have been married for over fifty-seven years, and we agreed that it would be a wonderful gift to go to heaven that way.

Warren laughingly said, "Why don't you go first. I'll see that you get the songs that you want at your funeral and give you a great send off."

"If you go first", I said, "I'll let everyone watch your old Gene Autry movies, while listening to country and western songs." We had no idea what the next two days would bring.

The next day I went to my water-walking class at the local YMCA. After the class, I began to have trouble walking. Getting to my car took a lot of effort. When I got home, I elevated my feet and legs and rested. Later the next day, my legs and arms began to swell.

Because it was a Saturday, I decided to wait until Monday morning to see the doctor, but by 7:30 that evening, I was filling up with liquid at an alarming rate. I asked Warren to call an ambulance, adding, "Please tell them not to use their lights and sirens, I don't want to entertain the neighborhood." Of course, I forgot about the fire department. They came with their big red truck, lights flashing, sirens blaring, attracting neighbors, from blocks away.

Not wanting me to see how worried he was, Warren joked, "We should have popped popcorn. We could have made some money."

I was able to walk to the gurney, and lie down. I remember looking up at Warren and my niece Ruth Ann, who lived next door and had come over when the Fire Department arrived. She was a big help to us during this ordeal. After that everything turned black. I arrived at the Stormont Vail Hospital emergency room in a coma, nearly DOA.

I was resuscitated in the emergency room and came to, only to realize that my body was shutting down. I could literally feel my life draining away. I heard both my niece and my husband say that my feet were black and my skin was pale gray. I could hear the doctors talking, trying to decide what was wrong with me. I knew I was not going to live, but I was not afraid. I told whoever was listening, to tell my husband I loved him, and to get hold of my son. And then I went into a death coma, and visited a wonderful place.

I was given a glimpse of heaven, many times during the next 8 days.

First, I was in a dark hallway, a tunnel of sorts. It was dark, but not pit black. I passed by a pit where I could hear crying and moans, but I did not stop to see what it was for I knew I was not interested.

I could see a light at the end of the hallway and a sheer curtain through which I could see persons moving about. I kept going towards them. I was never afraid, and when I got close I asked the figures why we had to have so many wars and killings on earth. Then I said, "I believe that Jesus was the Son of God. I believe in the Holy Ghost, but I could not remember the rest.

In a soft rhythm of threes, I heard what sounded like a train going over the iron rails, clickety-clickety-click, clickety-clickety-click. Voices kept repeating over and over in chant, "You live forever, you live forever, you live forever."

After what seemed a long time in the dark hallway, I cried out in despair, "Oh, don't tell me there isn't any heaven!".

Immediately a bright light surrounded me, filling the area where I stood. It was beautiful beyond description, so beautiful that it took my breath away. I'm not certain I can find the right words to describe it. Standing in the light made me feel whole, pure, blessed, free and loved. It was awesome. I wanted to bask in its energy and never leave. I felt I had just been born again into another realm, where I was completely at peace with my surroundings.

Again, voices told me that I would live forever and never die, that only my body would be left behind, and that I would get a new body. Three more things were revealed: 1. There were no clocks in heaven. My relatives would know when I was to come, and when I got there it would be as if I had been with them always.

This was impressed upon me as a very important fact. Only on earth would I feel the pain of separation. In heaven I would be just in another room. I could see my relatives, friends, and family anytime I wanted. 2. There was no money or wealth to be brought with me, since it was of no value there. 3. My position on earth was of no importance, because I would be glorified in heaven.

As I looked around me, to my left I saw a curtain. Shaped like a steeple, it was closed at the top and opened at the bottom. I could see people moving about beyond the curtain. There was a darkened area that I would have to cross over, and somehow I knew that I would probably not come back to earth if I went through the curtained area. On one hand, I wanted to go ahead, and yet I hesitated.

I wanted to go back and get Warren, so he could see this wonderful place too. I felt I needed to go back and help him on his way to this beautiful place called heaven. Warren has neuropathy in his legs and I felt he would need my help.

I knew I would be able to come back here in the near future, so I told them what I had in mind. I didn't hear a reply, so I continued to inquire if I could see my mother and father. I heard no reply.

I asked if I could see Warren's mother. I heard a voice from behind the curtain say, "Thank you for the ball and the cross," I didn't know what that meant then, but I would understand it later.

I knew that the ability to see what I was witnessing was a great gift, and I also knew that I would never have any fear of dying. What was waiting for Warren and me was more than wonderful.

When I awoke in intensive care, I was watched very carefully in case I slipped away again. After a couple of days, I awoke with a clear memory of what I had witnessed while away from my body.

I called my sister Joy, and told her, "You had better get up here, because Mom and Dad and all your brothers and sisters would be coming". I thought since I could see the angels, she could as well.

She hurriedly got dressed and came to the hospital. She said I was bubbly and happy. My niece and the nurse said I had awakened singing "Bringing in the Sheaves."

Everyone said they could tell that I had indeed seen something wonderful. My face was radiant. I told everyone who came to see me what I had seen. I kept singing, "I've got a secret, I've got a secret."

I could not understand why I had been the one chosen to see this glorious sight, why I had been given such a gift. My niece and sister were excited for me.

When I was still in Intensive Care, I was still having problems. The doctors put mirrors down my throat and put me on oxygen and a BIPAP machine to help my breathing. I was not expelling carbon dioxide, and that was poisonous to my system. One lung had been punctured, collapsed. In the process I died again.

This time I saw a skit put on for my benefit. There are no words to tell you what it was all about, but I can tell you about a woman dressed in a white dress with gold inserts who showed me how to get out of bed, so my back wouldn't be so painful. She told me her name was Mary, and that she had a nine-year old daughter.

Next, I was sitting in a marble room talking to my husband Warren, my son Bill, and my daughter-in-law Tammy. I remember the room quite vividly, and a voice in the background chanting. "You live forever, you live forever, you live forever".

I remember talking to the angels and asking them to tell my sister Joy that some angels do not have wings. I felt great peace with the angels. This visit was very brief. I remember waking back up in my room, and hearing the doctors say, "That was a close call".

For the first time in my life, I felt alive to the knowledge that I had gained on my journey into the other world. I then realized that you cannot go there unless you are ready to die.

Later, when I was transported to a room on the sixth floor, I was still in a trance, pondering what I had just witnessed. It was dusk when I awoke. A pretty Christian nurse stood by my bed. When I asked her name, I thought she said "Mary, Mary Rose."

"Oh," I said, "you are the mother of Jesus." She laughed and said that I was still on earth. I couldn't understand that. After all, I'd just been in heaven minutes before. Rose said that she was married to Michael, and that, they had three children. I guess that Joseph had died and she married again. She continued to assure me that I was, indeed, back on this earth.

After we had talked for some time, there was a woman who came from in back of the room, and stood to one side. I could see her as plain as day. She was standing in what I thought was her own expanded room area, as my hospital room was not that big. She wore her hair short, bobbed, and her dress was long, with those same gold pleats inserted in it. She wore a princess type top, and full skirt. She stood very quiet waiting.

I told the nurse that there was a woman behind her, and she answered that she had seen her before. I asked what did she want, and Mary Rose said she was waiting for me. After a few seconds, she turned to go back in the direction she had come. The only problem was that there was no door in the back of my room.

After a couple of weeks, a physical therapist came to exercise my legs. She told me her name was Mary, and I told her yes, and you have a 9 year old daughter. She seemed surprise as she had never met me before and wondered how I knew the age of her daughter. I told her I had met her down in ICU. She said that couldn't have been possible, as she and her daughter had just gotten home from California, where they had been for the past 2 weeks.

I continued to improve and was to stay until Aug 26th. I then was sent to the Rehab Hospital for 11 more days. When I called Mary Rose to thank her for the care of me in the hospital, she told me I had been given a great gift and I had also been very, very sick, at heaven's door more than once.

Remember the ball and cross that I mentioned? Many months later, my husband and I were looking at some old letters, written by his mother Esther, to her mother. The letter was dated early Jan 1929. In the letter, Esther thanked her mother and sister Minnie for the gold crosses they had given her for Christmas. Esther was pregnant, and was to have delivered a baby girl in the late July or early August of 1929. July 29th, she was accidentally shot and killed with an "unloaded" gun thrown carelessly on the bed. Killed with her was her unborn full termed daughter, Emma Ruth. When they were laid in the casket, the baby was wrapped in a blanket and put into her mother's arms. Around Esther's neck was a gold cross. When they had the visitation, Aunt Julie was holding Warren, who was 2 years old. In his hand he held a rubber ball. The only thing Warren remembers is his mother lying there, and he saw her, he reached for her, perhaps dropping his little ball. We both cried when we read the letter.

I have told everyone what I had seen. Even my doctor listened and thanked me for sharing this with him. He wanted to share it with his nurses and staff. He said it would make him want to be a better person. Everyone I have told always tell me how wonderful it makes them feel to know what is to come. Some cry in relief, some cry for happiness. But it always brings a smile to their faces and happiness to their hearts.

Warren has now told me that he too had seen the angel in the hospital, when I was taken up to my room. He said for a long time he could not believe that he saw her, but he knew after I repeated the story I told, that he did indeed see her. He saw her walk behind me and she just disappeared. We both feel everyday that her presence is still with us in our lives. It has changed our lives forever.

I have given this message out to many friends and relatives. I have sent it to New Zealand, Ireland, and Germany. It is now being passed around the United States. All I know is everyday I am thankful to him for letting me see what is to come. I feel I am far richer than I would be if I had won the lottery.

Four medical doctors have read my letter. Two have sent notes thanking me for sharing it with them. One doctor's wife had just died, and he too could verify that she did not leave this earth alone, as someone was with her. Another doctor sent me a letter and told me, "he wanted to be a better man", after reading my story. He left his practice, went back to his mother, telling her about the miracle. He returned to New York, to finish his education, with a new future.

PROCLAMATION: Some people call what happened to me an out-of-body-experience. I call it one of God's miracle mysteries.

After having read this story, everyone has now learned that earthly materials you have on this earth is of no value, only love of everyone is of importance. It cannot be bought, has no monetary value and is freely given a gift that is more valuable than life itself.

I have an excitement bursting inside of me that makes me swell with pride of what I was given as a gift into the other realm. It is there all my waking hours. It brings me peace.

We have a wonderful trip planned out for all of us in the future. Where you will feel when your earthly chains are taken away, and your heavy load will lighten. It is the most glorious feeling on earth.

Everyday we can feel our angel is near. But we will have to wait patiently for her to tell us when it is time to go.

WITNESSES: I have received rave reviews about my story. Some people have had the same experiences I had, but said I explained it in better detail. The nurse at the Hospice Hospital said that he enjoyed my book very much and that I had been privileged to have witnessed what is to come for all of us. He said some of his patients also saw what I saw before they left this earth. Only your body dies, and an angel is with you before your final separation from the body.

Some of the chapters were written out of sequence, because there were times I did not want to share all I saw. But pressure from beyond my understanding kept pushing me to tell all. That is why I awoke from a deep sleep singing "I've got a secret, I've got a secret". Everyone wanted to know what I had seen, and all I could do was beam and smile, and sing. It will all come out in Gods time.

TO WHOM IT MAY CONCERN: Enclosed are several more chapters of my Heavenly trip. Several people have encouraged me to continue with my story. One is the doctor, who knew that I had not told all there was to tell and so I will continue.

Since he deals with patients who are on the threshold to this glorious place, and who also reported seeing angels upon approaching their new journey, he should know. So much happened that sometimes it is hard to know where to start and when to finish.

I am amazed that I saw so much in such a short time, and yet it just all flashes back to me from time to time, and I will always remember it clearly. As you know, I saw Heaven not just once, but at many different intervals. Since I was in intensive care for 8 days, my life on this side was interrupted quite a lot. I came and went at will. I bustle with pride to be given such a gift, and it has changed my life forever.

I am not Catholic, but two priests, from Missouri and Kansas was praising me for my story, and encouraging me to continue. Other things I saw may never be told, because no one would ever believe it as well.

CHAPTER 2

"Being called to Witness

I do not know what "being called is" but I have a burning desire to continue telling what else I saw when I made this trip to Heaven. As I told you in the first chapter, you can see everything with an open mind and a broad view. Your eyes and mind take in so much that sometimes you are not aware of doing so, but it is there in your thoughts at a moments notice.

You feel excited yet always in awe. There is so much to tell, and even after I write this chapter, I will only be skimming over, some of the visions I have witnessed. Remember time is of no importance, so visiting this place surpasses all time zones. On earth I could have only been gone two or three minutes, yet in Heaven it was a very long time, or so it seemed to me. I seemed to have time at a stand still, where I could just wander along and take in all the sites.

The people, who have now read my first chapter, have encouraged me to continue with my story. Some have asked me great questions, like are there men and women, and can you tell them apart? The answer is yes, men are dressed in usually a robe. Where women are usually dressed in a billow like dress, it looks like airy gossamer.

If you remember I asked for my mother and father. I do not remember seeing them, but I must have because when I returned to intensive care the first time, I called my sister Joy to hurry and come because "your Mother and Dad were coming and all of your brothers and sisters.

I then asked to see Warren's mother Esther. I remember seeing her sitting just a few feet away. She was lounging on what I could describe as a marble bench. She had dark hair, wearing a dress that was light as air, which floated around her. Sitting next to her was a young blond child, who I took to be Emma Ruth.

Emma Ruth appeared to be somewhere in the ages of six or ten. They seemed happy and loving. I did not know either one on this earth, because they died in 1929, and I was not born until 1931. Emma Ruth was taken from her mother's womb, full term. That is why I do not believe that there are babies in heaven. I think that when a baby dies, their spirit leaves this earth as an older child. But that is my belief.

Cherubs might exist, as depicted in the Bible, but I did not see any. I only saw young children.

What amazed me so was the love that spilled out from everyone I saw. I can never repeat this enough.

Someone asked me, about suicides. I cannot tell you that, as the answers were not given to me. But my own understanding of it all would be that God wants you to live on his terms, and not end your life on yours. He did not promise that life would be easy for any of us, and we are to struggle everyday and take the good with the bad. I feel if you love your self and others that you will not end your life.

Someone asked me if I knew everyone I saw there? The answer is yes. You keep your own mind, except that all the ill feelings are gone. When you go through that white cloud everything is washed away. Yet you know who you are, who your parents are, who your friends are.

You remember all the good things, but the love is so absorbing in your thoughts that nothing else matters.

You can visit with your relatives and friends when ever you like, as they are always there. Since there are no clocks in heaven, the persons there think they just saw you, only on this side you have been separated.

Some people ask if you work, or just play? When I was in the darkened hallway, I saw persons moving things around. My husband laughed and asked about cardboard boxes. I don't know what they were moving, but they seemed bent over moving something. It takes no effort to work, or play. I think you have things to do and other places to see.

People asked if you look the same as on this earth? The answer is no, and yet, yes. You are not blood and muscle. You are as light as a feather, with slim appearances. You look like all humans, with eyes, feet, hands and hair on your head. But you do not walk. You just float along. You talk through your thoughts. They answer back through your thoughts.

I was asked if you kiss, or have sex. The answer is no. You remember your husband, but the sex on earth is a beautiful need of the body. In Heaven your body is beyond that kind of need. You get another kind of spiritual need from the love you emit from each other. That kind of love satisfies you beyond your wildest dreams. I don't think you touch each other because you are touching them spiritually. So you don't need to touch them personally. You will know your loved ones and enjoy their presence.

Someone asked me if it made any difference if they had been married twice. The answer is no, because you will visit and enjoy the best of everyone.

If you believe in a loving God and you are a good person, doing for others, loving others as you do your self, then with Gods blessings, I believe that you will be able to experience the same things I have seen.

I believe that judgment occurs immediately after you close the door to this world. I know for a fact that if you are evil you will be judged. You will go straight to hell. Because when you go through that wonderful white cloud and it washes your soul and makes you pure, you feel all that love that God has given you.

Why I saw Hell and heard the cries and moans, I do not know for certain. I feel now that it was so that I could come back and tell everyone there is certainly a hell. Since there are no clocks, if you are evil enough to go to hell, you will be there for all eternity.

The Lord has given me the knowledge to understand what I have seen and witnessed, to spread the word of his workings, and the gift that is to ours to come.

There are a lot of strange and wonderful things that are happening in our world, proof that there is a God, and he is great.

CHAPTER 3

"Questions and Answers"

When something like this happens to you, at first you cannot make any sense of it. I have asked numerous times. "Why me, Lord, what have I ever done to deserve this great honor?" I now know that an angel has been with me long before I took my last breath, she continues to be with me even to this day. She is so much a part of us. That some days it is hard to believe it, but we accept her as a blessing and a part of our home. She is my right hand, and guides me daily.

Warren had also seen her at the hospital, and he too has sensed that she is still with us every minute. We are aware that we can feel her presence as she guides us. She will guide our thoughts, so we can help everyone that is going through the valley of the shadow of death on the way to heaven. It is such a gift for everyone to receive, that we are in awe of her presence.

Sometimes she makes me get up at two or three o'clock in the morning because she doesn't know what a clock is. She makes me tell everyone what is to come. She's very bossy! But I do her bidding otherwise things happen to me that I cannot explain.

I opened the garage door the other night, but it kept going down by itself, so I opened it again, and again it went down by itself. I gave up and started writing my thoughts again. The next day I opened the garage door it worked quite well.

I also need to ask everyone for patience, I have so much to tell and so little time to tell it. The angel leaves me sometimes, and I do not know what she is up to, she may be napping. At least she probably catches up on her sleep, even if I don't.

I can not tell you enough, but when you leave this world, you will go into a new realm. It is very beautiful. It brings you peace. It makes all those chains of this world drop away. You do not realize how heavy some chains are until you get there and it is taken away from you. Stress, anxiety and despair are no longer part of your life. Only happiness, serenity and love are available.

That white cloud that you walk through takes all the weights off your body and mind, yet you are left with good memories, and a mind to think with. You do not remember yesterday but only tomorrow, and yet even though time is not important, you remember your loved ones. The love of everyone is so great that it seems to flow from your very person onto another person, and back around to everything and everyone.

Someone asked, can you look down and see earth? The answer is no. You don't want to look back and see where you have been. You are so excited that you want to just look ahead and see what else there is to come. On one hand I wanted to stay and take in the excitement and bask in that love, and yet I knew I would be back at a later date, so I reluctantly came back to this earth. I think it was that I was not in pain, and I did not mind returning.

Some persons who are hurt in an automobile accident, or shot, or have died tragically know it will be painful to put their souls back into their bodies. I had a job to do, to come back and take care of Warren. This had been quite a discussion between members of the Heavenly world, so it was decided I would return.

Later, when I came up to my room in the hospital with the guardian angel, she appeared in my room, and stood there so long, just waiting.

I thought she was there to see if I was alright, or she might have been there in case I changed my mind. I think she really wanted me to come with her, but she accepted the task at hand. I can still feel her drawing power on me, so I know time for me is getting short, and I have a job to do while I am here.

Some people have asked me about reincarnation. There are a lot of questions I cannot answer and was not given to me. This question I cannot answer.

There are some things I have seen that I still cannot describe them to this day, so I will have to wait until I return to my heavenly home. I look forward to this trip everyday. I am very excited about it, and I will tell you again and again, do not be afraid.

Everybody is here for a reason. Some people get their priorities mixed up. Some are selfish and desire wealth and comfort for themselves, while others have to struggle every day just to put food in their mouths, and do not know where they will sleep.

I know God does not want you to starve yourself, but he wants you to be willing to share the food you have. He wants you to have a roof over your head, but he also wants you to find a roof for others as well. He wants you to have clothes to wear, but he wants you to clothe other people as well. He wants you to have wealth, but he wants you to be willing to share your riches too.

I use to struggle with this myself and yet I thought I was not doing enough. I use to value what I have as property and trappings around me, but when I came back from the Heavens, I realized that everything I own in my house is of no value at all. It just collects dust, and is just for show.

If each of us would take one person who has fallen to the wayside and help them get on their feet again, to making a living, and supporting their families, and they in turn would help someone to do the same, what a wonderful gift this would be for all of us. It would fit into the plan of loving another one as your-self. The angel told me that you cannot bring wealth with you as it is of no value. So you might as well put it to good use while on this earth as it will be left behind.

I knew a family who had lots of money. Before the father died, he made arrangements for his wife, his 3 sons, 1 daughter, and himself to be buried in copper caskets, which costs $90,000.00. This money in God's plan would have fed ten poor families of four, for over seven years. The man did give to orphanages, which speaks better of him. But he was still trying to take his wealth to heaven.

Some people tell me that they do not want to leave their loved ones, but angel says to me, that your loved ones are with you in Heaven. To understand this you must remember that there are no clocks in Heaven, so time is not important. When you are ready to leave this earth, your loved ones who have gone ahead will come back for you and receive you as well. The ones left behind will be there before you have a chance to miss them.

What was interesting was I never did go completely into the Garden, and yet I was able to look into the Heavenly gates. Sometimes I went in for a quick peek, and other times I was on the outside looking in. It was like window shopping, up and down the block. Others have visited the Heavens and seen so much more than I have, and yet I saw quite a lot as well.

I was able to talk to people who were standing at the doorway of my new home. The invitation was very clear, and I was welcomed to enter, which I did want to very much. But discussions about me were going on all the time I was standing there. I guessed whoever was in charge of me, knew my outcome better than I did, so while I was window shopping, I let them decide what was best for me.

Something exciting is happening all the time you are there. You think that after you leave this earth, you will just lie in the grave, but that is so far from the truth that I want to climb up on the roof of my house and shout as loud as I can to everyone that, you don't have_to worry. Since your pain is taken away from you when you enter this new realm you will have work to do and things to see, and you will have new energy and feel the enjoyment of doing what you want.

Remember life on this earth is short for all of us. Looking back, it seems like I have lived a long time, but we have clocks here, which makes it feel as if time goes faster than it really does. Your life will mean nothing if you don't have anything to show for it, by loving others as your-self, and loving and believing in God.

It is light in heaven, with no darkness anywhere. I don't remember any shadows either. Some people ask about flowers, but I cannot remember actual flowers, but yet the surrounding is beautiful and colorful. I know in my mind's eye, that I would recognize it again, and remember it in full, but for now I cannot describe it to you. There was a domed building on the other end of the garden, I somehow knew that was the gateway into this heavenly Kingdom, but I did not go all the way in.

Some ask about singing and beautiful music. I heard something like that but my thoughts just blended it into my surroundings. I liked what I heard; it seemed to be music like, and yet more like, chanting. Had I gone further into the garden, I am sure I would have heard more of these sweet sounding voices.

Some people ask if just a few selected persons go, like some of the religions preach. God says no, all are welcomed, if you believe in me and repent. He says, "Go out unto the earth and preach my gospel. Love one another as I love you. There is room for everyone who comes to me". His heavenly home goes on, and on, and on. It stretches out forever, in all directions. There is room for all of us there. And I promise you, you will be happy there.

This has brought me back to the time when I was 10 years old. We had a Sunday school project in my class where we were to read the Bible from cover to cover. The King James Version, New Testament was more understanding to my young ears and mind. I loved to read. I would read it every chance I got all that summer, fall, and the next summer. I would read in the hayloft, hiding up in the trees, in the back seat of our old car, in the outhouse, and hidden between the covers of the Nancy Drew mysteries, so my brothers wouldn't make fun of me.

But I read it through from cover to cover, although it took two years. I found it to be very interesting, a mystery, a tragedy, and a love story all wrapped up into one. I wasn't so sure about the last book, called Revelations. That was too much for my young mind to take in, and it left me somewhat afraid. I wasn't sure I could handle the outcome.

But since my heavenly trip, I can see I was happy that I had spent my youth reading such an important book. It has come back full circle and is such a great book. Even though I could not understand much of what I was reading at that time. God has now granted me the knowledge to understand this beautiful message and story, and it is there for the asking, for all to read.

My beautiful niece Helen is dying of cancer, and has just a short time to live. She will find God's out stretched hands waiting for her during this time, as he is with her. Her guardian angel was sent to help her struggle through this separation from her body, and this earth. She will leave her body behind and get a new perfect body.

Her brother Duane, who left us seven years ago at the age of forty after his heart gave out; her brother Richard, who died as an infant; her sister Patsy; her father Dean; and her nephew Bryan will all be there to receive her. She will be escorted to heaven's gates, where she will hear the chanting in song, you live forever, you live forever, you live forever.

Believe me, for I know ----God is indeed great.

CHAPTER 4

"In and out of my body"

I know what I saw, but why I was chosen is still a mystery, and I know it will be made clear to me in God's time.

This story could go on forever and ever as the heavens are like that as well. It takes into account the more seriousness of how I entered back into this world from the other realm.

One thing I mentioned in my first part of the book was a mystery to how it all came about, and when I re-entered this realm. I realized the mystery had to be understood by my mind and my whole being, in order to make the trip worthwhile and believable. The gravity of it was overwhelming. At the time that I wrote the first chapter, I knew I could feel my body actually shutting down. I knew this was what it felt like to die, and that this was my end of life on this earth.

I lingered in and out of my body as if time no longer existed. I looked around and saw a man standing again in his own space, as my area in the emergency room was not that big. He stood quite straight holding a staff, like I had imagined a shepherd watching his flock. At first I thought he was a doctor dressed oddly and holding a saline bottle on a rolling staff, but upon closer inspection I saw it was not so. His robe was off white, with gold flecks in it. His hair was black and close-cropped. He was not looking at me, just standing like he was listening, and yet guarding all of us. I knew at that time he was not of this world.

I now know that you can see everything in a wide swath, not like the tunnel vision of this earth. The doctors were working over me, and yet I could still see this man standing there waiting. I was told much later by my new lung doctor that the emergency room had acknowledged that I was at the brink of death. They said that my organs were shutting down and spilling into my blood stream. The doctors took a chance and gave me heavy doses of insulin, to try to reverse this action. It worked, but it took its own sweet time.

When I was talking at the gates or curtain opening, I remembered that I had seen the man from the emergency room, standing in the garden and to my left. He was once again not directly looking at me, but listening and watching to what was going on around him. His staff was in his right hand, while in the hospital room it was in the left hand. It seemed odd that I would notice the difference. I think I was trying to establish whether it was all a dream or was real, but I knew without a second thought it was real, as I was separated from my body. Warren said later that this man was the one he saw in my hospital room, when I saw the female angel. So I realized later this male angel was always with me through all my travels in the other realm. You could see he was of authority, but in a peaceful way.

Some people have asked me if I thought it was God, and I said I did not think so. Some have asked me if it was Jesus, I again said I did not think so.

I do believe if I had asked to see the Mother of Jesus, I would have been able to see her. Because whomever I asked for I saw. I now know that Jesus will be at our side when we end this journey and travel up into the heavens.

The more amazing part of this chapter deals with my understanding what happened to me when I returned to this realm and to my body. When they put my oxygen and air pack on my face, my brain went through a transformation of some sort. I can only compare it to the defragmentation of files and folders on a computer. I could see the building blocks of my brain, all in colors of reds, yellow, blue and green re-stacking into piles. This went on for several hours, and I did not think it would ever end. It continued until I finally fell to sleep.

When I awoke many hours later I felt I had been born again. My mind took on a new knowledge of what I had witnessed away from my body. I knew I had been given a gift from the heavens, and our Lord. It was instilled in me that I was of very sound mind, more alert, more knowledgeable than I had ever been before, with more understanding of what I had witnessed. And that I would never forget what I had witnessed until I returned to my heavenly home.

Then again I died and left for the second time. I heard a doctor say to the nurse, "she will more then likely have some brain problems, and she might not recover from any of this". I saw a nurse shake his head that he understood, and returned to his desk. I quit breathing again, and again they had to resuscitate me. This happened again when I stopped breathing for the third time. Each time I returned with my mind as clear as a bell, with no out side influences clogging my mind. My mind had erased all the evil thoughts, and my bad memories were gone. I am a new person, in tune with God's love and the love of everyone. Nothing else matters.

I think many people get chosen for this most wonderful experience, and I am one of the lucky ones. It has changed my life forever. There is never any anxiety or fear now. My belief in a higher being has always been there, but to see it and feel it so vividly is unforgettable. Sometimes I am so giddy with happiness about what I saw on the other side that I want to hurry along there. I love my husband, and my family, and have enjoyed my life as I know it, but I am also getting old. I realize that this new realm is closer than we think, especially for my husband and me.

I hope that through this book, I have shared with you, a knowledge that all is well with the Lord, if you live your gift of life to the fullest with love, as God would want you to, and love everyone as yourself.

CHAPTER 5

"Angels abound"

This angel who is around and about us in our daily lives will have to send me a clear signal about what I need to do with all this information. I know I saw quite a bit more on my trip to the heavens, but my mind cannot remember it all, and some of the things I saw were indescribable. I have faith in her that she will let me know in due time.

Even though I want to hurry and leave this earth, she tells me in no uncertain way, that I am not to try to go ahead of my time. That we are all on this earth for a reason, and we are to go about our lives remembering that we are God's children, of which we answer just to him, and do as he asks. There are a lot of jobs left undone, and we are meant to find what they are and do them in God's name. Life is so precious to all of us, but we are not to just stand by, and watch the poor, the sick, and the desperate, starve, struggle, and weep in despair. We might be in the same boat ourselves someday, and we need to love them and ease their suffering. Every act of kindness transforms the world around us with its beauty and light.

Chapter 6

"The Shining City"

I have held off about telling everyone about the city I saw. I felt that it was such an amazing event that it was almost too much to take in. It was one of the marvels that surprised me, and I wasn't sure anyone would believe it. I felt I had witnessed a secret, that only the angels and I have shared a gift from the heavens.

Remember there is no time, but there is distance. I saw the heavenly city when I came out from the cleansing white cloud. It set far off in front of me. If I had to guess, it seemed to me to be two miles away. My sister Joy asked me if there were sky scrapers and bridges; there were not. It was nestled close to what we would call ground.

A lot of the buildings were domed, with golden colors, white like ivory and pearls, and gray like marble. It was the way that it sparkled and shone in the light that drew my attention. It seemed to be spread out, over what I would call many miles. I feasted on its beauty for some time, realizing that this was what I would have when I returned from earth. The very fact that it existed assured me that all would be well for all of us. That we would never miss what we had on this earth and that we would never want to go back once we were here.

I awake every morning savoring in the miracles that I witnessed that wonderful day in August. To everyone else it may have been a sad day, but I was given great gifts from God and his angels.

After you have served your time on this earth witnessing for the Lord, and after reading my book, you will be as happy as I am, from knowing what God will be giving to you as well. I will have to wait patiently now, for the angels to remind me that there are more things to tell. I have been assured that God and his angels will look after you, and I am a witness that they are with you, all the days of your life.

Chapter 7

"The Gate"

This chapter is really a recap, to try to cover what I missed, when writing the first part of the book.

In looking back, and putting the pieces together, I feel that after you go through the white cloud and your soul is cleanse, that you will see that beautiful city beyond.

You will have to go through the filmy curtain, then into the garden gate. Your friends and relatives have come and welcomed you in. Then you will go through the domed building and on into the Eternal City.

The Eternal City is way beyond the garden, but yet you have the ability to see it off into the distance. Its buildings gleaming in the light.

You will glide everywhere. What is beyond the city must be more than wonderful, treasures beyond your wildest dreams. Nothing down hear on earth is of any value.

Dreams are a part of our earthly life, but I knew what was happening to me was not a dream. I was separated from my body and looking back at what was going on around me. I was past feeling any pain, and yet I knew they were prodding me, and sticking needles in my body, using the paddles, trying to make me respond.

The incidents that I described in all my chapters are branded into my memories, and I can remember them clearly everyday. They will be there for all eternity.

I know when I return to this heavenly place, I will recognize and remember everything I saw, and I will know that I have been there before.

I knew each time I took in all the sights, that time was endless, and yet I knew I did not have time to tarry. My mind was like a sponge soaking in everything around me. The persons I saw at the gate were familiar and yet I cannot put a name or a face to them. They were excited that I was there, and I knew they wanted me to come in. They were happy and laughing and they emitted lots of love towards me.

The first building past the gate and beyond the curtain was large in structure, and again I noticed it was made of granite. It had large openings for windows, and it is odd that I would notice there were no screens. Everything was open with no obstructions. There were wide opened doorways, but no doors that shut. Yet I took time to notice the domes of ivory.

The city was further off in the distance, but this large building was just beyond the gate.

People have asked me if you wear shoes, and all I can say is, I did not see any. You don't need them because your feet never touch whatever the brown area below your feet is made of. You float from here to there, yet you move your legs. But the male angel I saw later was walking in the garden clearly on a path.

I have been asked about glasses, and you see everything with your mind, but you have eyes and look out of them. You look like human beings as we are on this earth.

Some people ask about food, but I do not know what the Bible means by the feast at the banquet table, where all your relatives gather. I was not told how or what the body is made of, or how it works, all I know is you are as light as a feather, and you just glide right along. I did notice how light you feel there, without the chains of life you have to carry here on this side.

As you read and enjoy this book about my trip to this beautiful realm, you will understand that I was only given a peek into what is to come for all of us. I have written this book to share with you this gift God and his angels has granted me to see.

Everyday you must thank God that he has gone and prepared a home for us. Our old bodies are made to wear out, and our new bodies will last forever.

Heaven is your reward, and God loves us all.

CHAPTER 8

"The angels never leave us"

I t is amazing. The angels are with you from the beginning to the end of your journey. They welcome you in song, rejoicing with out pouring love. You never feel alone or afraid. You are drawn to their power, and yet they only guide you. You want to follow them because the love they give you is so overwhelming. It is more of a chant, like a beckoning on the breeze.

I never saw any angels with wings, but I would not be surprised to find some. I wished I had, so maybe I would be able to understand the difference. There is a difference between the men and the women. As I have said before, the clothing dress is different. The male Angel was very serious and I only saw the same one twice that I remember. With the women Angels, which there were several, were very friendly and excited, ready to welcome you into their fold. Love is everywhere, and it draws you into everything.

The people I saw at the gate were not angels, and the fact that I knew the difference at the time surprised even me. Even the ones I saw at the end of the hall way moving things around, I don't think were male angels. I have tried to rack my memory for many nights, in the peace of my bed, trying to place who the ladies at the gate were but I cannot remember. I know they were familiar, but their names elude me. They knew me, but I could not remember them.

The persons I saw at the gate were always beckoning me to come in. I knew them but I could not put a face to them. I still see them in my mind yet, and someday I feel it will come to me.

There was also a man standing outside the gate and away from the women, smiling as if he knew me. Then I realized that if God had wanted me to know who they were, someone would have told me.

Later, I questioned my thoughts on Mary, the Mother of Jesus. I had been talking to her, but I cannot remember what it was about. I cannot get this clear in my head or my memory. When I came awake later in the Intensive Care Unit, I asked the nurse if she was Mary, the mother of Jesus. She smiled and said she was not, yet I can remember clearly of seeing Mary earlier, sitting on a smooth stone bench, smiling.

I told the nurse what I saw, and she said that I probably had seen her, as I had been in heaven and near heavens door several times for the last eight days. The staff and nurses were very watchful of me during my ordeal.

Warren, my husband said the line on monitor went flat several times, then the alarm bell would go off, and the blue light code would sound, and everyone would come running. He said it had happened so many times, that the staff quit asking him to leave. My bed had been located right next to the nurse's station. They asked several times if Warren wanted a minister to call on me. Warren was trying to prepare himself for what was to come. He told me later that he could feel an unseen presence during my near death experience. He knew that the angels were watching over all of us. I am sure they never leave the ICU area for very long.

At that time I never thought about Lot's wife. I did not want to come back for my own gain or loss. I wanted to come back and help Warren, so he could come with me to this other beautiful realm. I was ready and willing to stay, if that was what was expected of me to do.

I wished I had had more of a lingering conversation with my mother and father. This is something that I cannot grasp. Yet I know I saw them, but it is so vague and elusive now. Some people say that they would like to see their mother again, and I say "Look in the mirror". I can see my mother looking back at me many times. I enjoy this very much, and I am able to convey my thoughts to her. She was a very good Christian lady and a loving person as well. She guided us all with the help of the angels.

As you read this book about the trip to this beautiful realm, you will understand that I was only given a peek into what is to come for all of us. I have written this book to share with you this gift that God and his angels have granted me to see.

I wake up happy and go to bed happy, knowing what I know. I do indeed have a secret.

Every time I would wake up from my bed, I found someone nearby hoping I would be able to tell them something more. My mind and thoughts were very full, and yet I felt I could recount it over and over.

Even my minister said he understood my sightings, and he believed they were true. He nodded his head and agreed that I had witnessed something remarkable. I could not believe that I had been so blessed.

All who came into my room said something marvelous was happening, and it was a miracle that I was alive to tell it. My heart and voice sang out constantly. My happiness was overwhelming, and it almost left me breathless. But my breathing machine took care of most of that.

Thank you God for letting me see and tell what is to come for all of us.

Everyday you must thank God that he has gone to prepare a home for all of us. Our old bodies are made to wear out, and our new bodies will last forever.

SECTION II

"True Stories of Miracles in our lives with angels and Christian love."

CHAPTER 9

"Mother's Visit"

Warren and I have had many miracles in our married life. I never took any of them for granted and was in awe and felt blessed that these things took place in our lives.

Warren's uncle Karl was a missionary in Nigeria, Africa in 1938. He and his wife Thekla lived in a small village there. One evening, on November 17, 1943 at 6:30 in the evening they were hoeing their garden. Thekla was about twenty five feet away from Karl, when she heard voices. She thought someone had come to visit them. When she looked up from the ground where she was weeding, Karl was smiling and talking to someone, but there was no one about.

Thekla called out and asked, "Who are you talking to?" He replied, "My mother". Thekla arose and went to him. His face was a beam of light, and he was smiling and happy. She could not see anyone around, yet the great smile on his face was enough to tell her that he was seeing someone and feeling a presence about him. They later went into the house and talked and thanked God for such a gift.

It always took six weeks for packets and mail to reach Africa from Holton, Kansas and when the mail arrived next, Karl found out that his mother Elizabeth had passed away on November 17, 1943 at 6:30 in the evening Nigerian time. God is indeed great.

Chapter 10

"My brother's and their angel"

This reminds me of when my brother Lee died. Dying was a blessing for him because he had a rare form of infectious rheumatoid arthritis. He was in severe pain and was bedridden.

The day the angel came for him, I was sitting besides his bed and gently talking to him. It was late afternoon. While I was looking at his face and eyes, I noticed a veil come down over his eyes, and the eyes that were once watery were now dull with no life in them. He was still with me, but his time was short. I had never in my life seen anything like it, and I have asked several ministers, and doctors why this happens, but they had never witnessed that themselves and could not answer me. I knew someone was there with him that I could not see, as he seemed more at peace and at rest.

I lost my other brother Mark five months later to lung cancer. He lived in West Virginia. My sisters and family traveled there to see him in his last days. When we got there, we saw that his days on this earth were numbered. I visited with him several times, and the night before we left, I was alone with him in his room. When I went in, he was smiling and talking to someone there. I asked him who he was seeing, and he smiled and said, "Lee is here and getting impatient. He said to hurry up, as he has things to do, and placed to see." He said, "I can hardly wait for the angels to take me. I wish they would hurry."

Remember, time is not important

CHAPTER 11

"Changing Churches

Warren had been raised in the Evangelical church, and I had been raised American Baptist. We were married in his church and stayed with his religion for our first years of marriage.

Both churches led to God, so it made no difference to us which one we attended. Warren's uncle, Karl and great uncle Christopher were both ministers of the Evangelical church and were a guidance in his life. He and I had known Christ all our lives, so we had the best of both worlds before us.

We moved to Topeka and settled in the Evangel United Church. When our son Bill was born we soon found out that he would not have brothers and sisters. Warren and I decided that we would take foster children into our home. This was a miracle for all of us. It gave our son Bill playmates and gave the children a loving home.

While attending the Evangelical church, we found something lacking in our lives at that time. Warren was a city fireman and had days off, so he took to building houses. We had built a large house for our family in the country. One day, as he was driving down the street she noticed a small Baptist church that looked like it needed some help with painting, mowing the large yard, and some carpentry work. He came home and asked if all of us wanted to go to another church for a while. It sounded like fun, and we all attended the next Sunday. We found a great reception. But Warren said he needed to pray about this before he joined for good.

One night, months later, Warren woke up suddenly. He was used to waking at odd times of the night, because he slept in the watch office at the fire station when on duty. Thinking he was at the fire station, he arose, and looking out of the window by our bed, he saw a man sitting on a large rock below our window in the garden area, about twenty feet away from Warren. He wore a robe with a hood. He was smiling and nodding his head up and down. Warren was so surprised that he could see his uncle Karl that he called me to me to come and see. I got up and looked out the window. I could not see him, but I knew Warren had seen him, by the look on his face in the moonlight. His face was serene and at peace.

Chapter 12

"Our family miracles"

We had been attending this small Baptist Church for some time, when one day in Sunday school, we were just fooling around and we got into a discussion about belief in God. Was the Bible really real, or was it fiction written for the times? Was there really a God after all? We all just laughed and said we needed to test this theory. We were all a bit skittish about this testing, so when I prayed I asked for just a little miracle. Not a big jolt, but just a little nudge to prove to me once and for all if he did indeed exist.

I had been read to and preached to all my life and I wanted to believe in everything, but I just needed a little peek. My faith was being tested, oh woman of little faith.

My children knew this has been discussed, and they seemed to have more faith than I did, as they warned me that something terrible would happen. Maybe the world would end, their house would burn down, or God would get mad and strike me down, and then they would not have any more Mother. We promptly forget about it.

Several months later, we had decided to go to the Aunties house in Holton for Sunday dinner. We skipped church as it was forty miles north. It was a beautiful day. The sun was shining, and there was not a cloud in the sky. We had a truck with a shell on it and a window between the cab and camper shell. We talked and discussed the fun we would have that day on the farm.

We left town about ten thirty in the morning, and after driving for forty-five minutes, we stopped at the cemetery on the way to the farm, to check on the graves of all of Warren's relatives, including his mother, Esther, and Emma, his grandparents, and his father. We then continues on, and about one mile from the farm, all of a sudden from out of nowhere, the sky started getting terribly dark and wind buffeted out truck. Warren could not keep it on the road, and he was afraid it would overturn. It got even darker in a very short time, and we knew we could not reach the last mile home. We pulled into the driveway of the neighbor, and with some effort, we ran for their back porch to take cover.

There were cars about, but after repeated knocking, we could not get anyone to answer the door. We opened the glassed-in back porch and took shelter, yelling all the while for someone to answer us, but to no avail. I saw that potatoes were cooking on the gas stove, with flames licking up, almost engulfing the frying pan. I was afraid that the handle would catch on fire, so I walked into the kitchen and turned the fire down very low.

I continued to shout out for someone to answer us, but no one did. We all wondered if the owners were in the basement, waiting out the storm and were afraid to answer us when they heard the tromping of twelve feet on their porch. We must have sounded like cattle had gotten loose in their house. I did not think they would have forgotten their potatoes frying on the stove.

When the winds began to quiet down, we all left and drove on to the farm. The children were crying from fright and berating me for testing God. They made me promise that I would never ask for a sign again. When we got to the lane that the farm was on, the sky had turned blue again and we saw Aunt Minnie coming from the chicken house. The children were all excited and asked Minnie if she was frightened by the storm. She seemed surprised at the question. She said she had been out feeding the chickens and there was not storm around. The sky, she had noticed, was a beautiful blue and clear as a bell. She was only one-half mile away and would have noticed the dark clouds. Warren chimed in with the children and let me know they were not happy with my testing God. To this day, they never let me forget it.

Chapter 13

"God has a plan"

God and his angels have a plan for all of your lives. You might try to deny it, but whether you like it or not, it follows you wherever you go. And now that we are growing old, and looking back, we can see the plan much more clearly.

We had wanted lots of children, and we soon had them. We were never sorry to open our home up for all our foster children. We had lots of fun.

Our first child was a special gift we received from God. He was everything anyone could wish for, a bouncing blue-eyed baby boy, who was forever ours. He was our little miracle; The second, third, fourth, fifth and sixth ones were neighborhood children whom we helped get through their kindergarten years to their teens.

We had the enjoyment of practicing on them to help us in our later years. They had their own parents who picked them up at night. But they still remain our friends.

God wasn't through with us yet. I must always remember that he has a plan.

We then decided to take in children who would not leave us at nightfall. This changed our lives considerably.

All of us took a vacation every year, to learn about other people and animals and the wonderful land that God gave us to use. We have never regretted taking them into our home. They have all grown into wonderful adults, and have families of their own. We have been rewarded with eight grandchildren, and five great grandchildren. What an enjoyment and a miracle.

CHAPTER 14

"Christian Fun"

I don't want you to think that just because this is a church, you cannot have fun, because that is not so. We had a lot of fun attending both Sunday school and church.

We all got together for meals. We planned and painted the outside of the church, and repaired some of the bricks. We assigned people and the children for clipping the weeks, and keeping the extra large lot mowed. Then we set about getting families involved in coming to join us.

We sold candles one year to make extra money so we could buy and put down a carpet in the entry-way to make the entrance quieter upon approaching the sanctuary.

The ladies of the church had a garage sale for the church, which was lots of fun. It lasted two days, and the second day, we were able to get rid of nearly everything, when a student from Kansas University came by and we gave him a small table, one lamp, a kitchen chair, some dishes, an easy chair, and other assorted items for free. He was driving a VW, and he couldn't see how he could get it all in his car. But never fear when Christians are at work. The angel showed us how we could do it.

We removed his back seat, and put all the stuff he was taking in where the seat came out. It took some packing and re-arranging, and then we roped the car seat to the top of his car. We took a picture of it because we could not believe we had accomplished this. All of us including the young man prayed that God would let him get back to his dorm safely, and then we sent him merrily down the road. We closed the garage sale because everything was gone. We never heard from him again, so we trusted in the angels that he had reached home safely.

We took all the children and some of their friends to Worlds of Fun in Kansas City, Missouri several times. One time we started home with one too many little boys. We had counted heads, but another one of my group got into the wrong car, and I did not know it. So I had the right count, because another little boy joined up with our group, and was having so much fun, he didn't want to leave our group. I discovered this problem when someone mentioned it, and we had to turn around and take him back to Worlds of Fun and his parents. The exchange was made and after we got the children switched. I made everyone identify them-selves and vouch for each other before I left the park. Some of the boys had been a stranger to me, and it was hard to identify them when we started home.

The next year, we drove all the children and their friends to Summer Retreat in Colorado. We played campfire games, sang songs, went on hikes in the mountains, slept in cabins, and learned how God plays a part in our daily lives.

Every year for seven years, we put on a Christmas nativity scene. Now that was a treat. It made everything worthwhile.

We hunted around and found a very gentle donkey from one of the daycares in town. The men from the church had built a stable, and we built a manger and got some hay and straw from the farms. We put up a bonfire and lights.

We borrowed two sheep from a farmer nearby, a ewe and her lamb. We had a truck with sideboards, and we needed the help of all our children. The sheep were another story. If you have ever been around sheep, you will understand when we say that they went everywhere but where we wanted them to go. We just had to lift them up once we caught them and carry them to the bed of the truck. The lamb was sure to follow. Loading them up to take them home was also a problem, but we had strong men around to help.

The sheep never did get the idea to run into the bed of the truck, when we went after them. They would run all over the place, no matter what we wanted them to do. My children looked forward to trying to catch them. We would laugh for days after that. The next year, the children were ready to go again to help. I imagine the angels were laughing as well.

The second year we were spoiled with the gentle donkey, because we had to switch to a wild, stubborn one the following year, and had difficulty getting him loaded. This again took help from the angels, but we can accomplish everything with this extra help. We needed a long stick, a halter, and a very long carrot.

We used the wild donkey for several years, and we think he finally got the idea of what his job was, near Christmas. He was always waiting for us by the gate, but he still did not like the truck without the carrot.

One of the ladies who had a friend in the Shriners found that they had some old long velvet dress gowns that the organization had worn for their ceremonies. They wanted to get rid of them, so we took them and they worked out great. The wise-men were dressed in finery.

We performed for five nights. Some nights it was very cold.

We all just relied on the bon fire to keep us warm and toasty.

Warren was a fireman for the city, and he was in charge of watching the bonfire, to keep it safe and keep us warm. The adults and the children enjoyed our efforts, and it brought the meaning of Christ's birth and his angels to them.

My children still to this day remember that time in our lives, and wish their children could experience the same thing. Times change for them, but they are happy doing their own things, I am sure. I remind them that the angels are waiting for them to open their hearts and let God in.

Chapter 15

"My father and his Angel"

My father George had been raised in a Christian home, but he had been orphaned at the age of three. His father was a deacon in his church, and was a widower with four children to rear. He needed to find another wife to help him take care of his family.

My father was the youngest one born to Carroll and Charity Thompson in 1872, just about six years after the Civil War. He was born in a small settlement called Spirit Mound, near Vermillion, South Dakota.

His father and two brothers and one sister drove the team and wagon to town to buy supplies. His mother Charity, along with my father who was a baby at that time, was left at home. Charity heard shouting from far away, and when she looked out the windows of the farm house, she saw Indians coming towards the homestead. She was very frightened, but she found her courage and gathered up my dad.

After letting the farm animals out of their pens, she went down to the creek, getting into the water, and hiding under a large hollow tree stump. She nursed my father to keep him quiet. She told her husband later that she could see the bare feet of the Indians walking along the edge of the creek, searching for her. She stayed until it was dark and cold and then she crept out of the water and returned to the house. She could not start a fire to get dry, for fear of the Indians being close at hand, so she sat awake in a chair all night until her husband returned the next morning. God was looking after them. A miracle they survived. After this incident, Grandfather sold his home and moved his family back to Alton, Illinois. Grandmother Charity was never well after that, and she later died from being out all night nursing my father in the cold water.

My Grandfather Carroll kept the older children and gave his sister Caroline, my father to take care of. She was Catholic. She kept George until he was about six, and then George went back to live with his father and his father's new wife Jennie, who was born in Switzerland and spoke broken French.

They saw that George had the opportunity to attend college in Alton, Illinois. He took French and art. He was a great painter of portraits and was skilled at sketching. He also took up wallpapering and painting. He is well known as the artist who painted the angels and cherubs in the high, large ceilings of the train station, and churches, in Alton, Illinois.

My dad's brother Anson, who was seven years older than he was, was murdered at the age of fifteen while helping to feed the hoboes down at the river's edge in Alton, Illinois. His body was never found, but the man who murdered him was caught. He was given a life sentence and died in the federal prison in Leavenworth, Kansas.

My father was nearly twelve, and after Anson's death, his life changed. He was restless and unsettled. He was seventeen when he finished college. He traveled extensively, working on a ranch in Arizona, breaking horses and herding cattle.

Dad had a friend of long standing traveling with him. Dad drew up plans for a table with a wheel in the middle that held the sugar, salt and spices. His best friend stole his plans and made lots of money on it. He never gave my father any credit or any money for the invention. From then on, my Dad never gave away any of his ideas, and he had many.

At the age of twenty-two, he married his cousin. After seven children, and a troubled relationship, they called it quits.

In February 1917, at the age of forty-five, he met and married my mother Hattie. My mother was told at the age of sixteen, by a doctor, that she would never have any children. She had never planned to get married, so she stayed home and took care of her ailing mother. My mother was twenty-nine years old when she met my father, who had come to their house to decorate and paint it. My father was smitten with her and delighted that she could not have any children. He already had seven of his own, and he did not need any more. They both wanted to tour the world.

My dad could do just about anything to make money, so supporting his new wife was not going to be a problem, while they traveled. He had been a painter, a motorcycle police officer, a contractor, a farm hand and a ranch hand. He could do anything he put his mind to, and knew it. He thought he had the world at his fingertips, but God had other plans for him.

In December 1917, his first son Carroll, from my mother, who was his second wife, was born in Shenandoah Iowa, so much for well-set plans.

Then in 1919, Margaret was born in Oregon. She died three weeks later in Idaho.

Another daughter was born in 1920 in Georgia. In 1922, another son Lee, was born in Texas, and another son, Mark, was born 1923 in Asheville, North Carolina. Carroll got sick and died in Asheville. Daughter Joy was born in 1926 in Topeka, Kansas, and son John was born in 1927 in Olympia, Washington. Finally, I was born in 1931 in Benton, Arkansas. To let you know that God does have a great sense of humor, we were all born in different states. God is probably still chuckling about this one. He helped put many miles on my father's old car.

My father was fifty-nine years old when I was born. I think he had been praying for the population explosion to end for many years, but nobody was listening. God finally did answer him in 1931.

I still look back and wonder what they would have done without me. It's a question that I ask ever so often, but everyone just smiles.

My father had a lot of sins to resolve by this time, but God and his angels were still looking out for him and gave him a sign. Soon after, he joined the Odd Fellows and Masons. They were secret societies, but it was my understanding that they studied the Bible and believed in God. I was always listening around the doors and through the keyholes to find out what they were about, but my parents always seemed to know when ears were listening, and they would just talk softer. I finally gave up.

My father and mother always saw that we attended church from the time we arrived on this earth. We could only miss Sunday school and church if we were sick. My father did not attend Sunday church, but he and my sister would always go together on Wednesday night. He was like a guardian angel, always watching, always trying to keep us on the straight and narrow. None of my brothers ended up in jail, but I am assured they did get scolded by police officers several times. If it looked like they might be heading the wrong direction, they seemed to be enlisting in the navy the next day. All served their country, without getting killed in the war. They all married and raised their families, so my mother and father had a lot to be thankful about from the Lord.

My mother was a saint in her own rights and practice, and I am sure my father before his death had resolved his issues with God and his angels.

On the night he died, December 16, 1949, when I was eighteen years of age, my mother and I nursed him at home. He was dying of cancer. We soothed his mouth with ice cubes, to take away some of the pain. He said that the angels were coming for him.

He said he saw an angel all dressed in white, standing on the platform on the back of a train. He heard a whistle and knew it was time to go. The train was going down the tracks that crossed our land about a quarter mile away. We listened but could not hear the whistle. The tracks had been abandoned many years ago, and were broken and missing rails. My mother and I went to stand by the window, and we saw a ray of light, large enough to fit on the front of a train, waving back and forth going down the tracks. We then heard what sounded like a whistle. We could not understand what we saw, because there were no explanations for it to happen like that. There were only farm fields and grazing land around the tracks.

My mother and I checked in town the next morning to see if the train tracks had been repaired, but they were still broken up. A man at the all night gas station had also heard a train whistle far off in the distance, late in the evening. He too was surprised to hear the sound.

My father left us a short time later, with the broadest smile on his face. He seemed to glow with pride about where he was going and who he was going with. To witness this face-to-face, even though I was sad at his leaving us, I knew he was with the Lord most high, and the angels were taking him home where he belonged. I learned that night that we had just borrowed him for such a short time. What a miracle.

Chapter 16

"God and his angels"

Our small Baptist church was not growing as we would have like it to. We were able to get lots of children to come, but their parents would drop them off and then go back home. We tried several things to encourage the adults to attend as well, but we could see it was going to be an uphill battle. This battle had been going on since the beginning of time, but we all thought we could make a difference. The bigger churches were drawing in the adults because they were more beautiful and quite large. They had more money to work with as well.

We had also been set back because we started losing a lot of our older members. Some went on to heaven and some to other churches. I guess they could see the handwriting on the wall, but our family did not want to give it up. We tried everything we could think of. We sent out flyers and put up posters. We then lost our minister and his wife, who moved back east. They were going back to college to teach. We were then without a fulltime leader. We finally had to concede that God had other plans in mind and we would have to change our plans as well.

Warren was a deacon and was saddened that this church would probably end here, we would have to close down our church, and move somewhere else or merge with another. Our children were all leaving the nest, and moving out.

We became members of the First Baptist Church, which had one thousand members. Our son Bill and his wife Tammy were married in this church, which made us proud.

It also gave us a chance to rest for a year and re-build our energies.

Somehow we always found the strength with the help of God and his angels. We look back and realize we could not have done anything without their help. We don't know how anyone can live without God. I had a chance to go to Green Lakes Wisconsin, for a seminar, with other Christians. I think God was giving me a chance to rest and enjoy other people.

When I came back, Warren and I were made head of the local missions.

In looking back on our lives, we know that we would never have succeeded without the Lord and his angels. God has made everything possible for our very existence. With out him we are nothing.

Chapter 17

"The Heavens Open Up"

My sister Joy told me the night her husband Dean died, he was lying in bed, and it was after midnight. They knew he was pretty sick, and had been sick for some time. Dean did not want to go to see a doctor. He just refused to have someone look at him. Joy was sure that he had cancer, because he was in so much pain. But he still refused to go, and said he had a right to die at home if he wanted to. Then he agreed with her, that she was probably right, and he was sure it had already gotten a head start and gone too far. He knew for sure he did not want to die in the hospital. They let him have his wishes and he stayed at home.

All of his family was trying to help him as best they could, but he refused their help. They still would come in and out most of the day, to check on him. He was sleeping almost all the time and there was nothing they could do for him but give him pain killers.

Joy had to continue to work, since the only income they had at that time was hers.

When she came home, the night he died, she drove her car into the garage. After carrying her purse and things into the house, she came out and shut the garage door, as she turned around she noticed one bright light like a streak of fire shooting up from the roof of the house, over the room where her husband was sleeping, and rising up into the sky. She just thought it was a falling star, until she realized that it was going the wrong way.

She hurried into the house to check on his room, but he seemed quiet, so she thought he was peacefully asleep. She still could not understand what she had seen, but she settled down on the day couch, and soon dropped off to sleep. When the morning came, she went in to check on him, but he was gone.

She remembered that thin light going up into the sky and told the doctor about it when he came to pronounce him dead. He agreed that strange and wonderful things do happen when the departed leave this earth. The angels have a way of helping the souls on their way. The doctor said Dean had died about one a.m. in the early morning. He said he wouldn't be surprised if that was Dean's soul departing this earth, and going on to the next one. He is now at peace.

CHAPTER 18

"*A mother's return*"

A doctor friend of mine told me a story about when he lost his wife at such an early age. She was only in her mid-fifties when she starting having heart problems. It was too soon for her to die; after all she still had her whole life ahead of her.

She soon found out that there was no way she could get any help, because of the progressive disease.

She was in the hospital by then, and time was getting short. Her husband was sitting by her bed. She started to smile, and then she told her husband not to worry. She was going to heaven, and her mother was coming for her.

Her husband told me that he could feel, but could not see a presence that was around them. He knew someone else was there that was not of this world. He saw his wife's hand lift up and knew her mother had probably come to get her, as she seemed now at peace and happiness.

Chapter 19

"Her faith never wavers"

I had a friend, who had a young daughter that was coming upon her teen years. She had never been sick, except for colds, and the general diseases of childhood. The young girl was looking forward to her sixteenth birthday. She was a happy child, and so full of life. She had a secret that she did not want to share with her mother. The young girl had been having sharp pains in her side.

After suffering for a couple of weeks, she gave up and told her. Her mother immediately called their family doctor, who asked them to come in and he would run tests. The news was bad and it was as he suspected, that she waited to long. The cancer had gotten ahead start, and nothing could be done to stop it.

The daughter took the news quite well. She told her mother that she had been feeling the angels around her and were watching over her for some time. She seemed to accept the fact that she would be going home to heaven.

Her mother was feeling wonderful, that with all her teachings and reading the bible to her daughter that she had already prepared her for this journey.

Her mother would not show her grief now, but she would help her daughter prepare for her trip to this beautiful place. The doctor told them both that they had time to travel if they wanted to. That she would go peacefully in her sleep, no matter where she was, and so they set off on a cruise.

They went to Italy, and France, visiting the Alps. After about thirty days of wandering around Europe, the daughter died peacefully in her sleep.

The mother told me when she came home, that she had buried her daughter in a grave yard in Switzerland, where she had wanted to be buried. She told me she was so happy to have had her daughter, who was a gift from God. That God had just loaned her to us for a little while.

What a wonder faith they both had, to realize that we are all loaned out, and that God is truly our father, who art in heaven and to realize, you live forever.

PRAISES:

I have given this book out to many of my friends who have thanked me for sharing it with them.

Some have already lost their loved ones. I have been told that it brings them peace, comfort, and hope.

Let me tell you, my dear friends, there is always an angel with you as you leave this world. If you love everyone as yourself, the heavens will open up and receive you. But be aware. If you are evil with evil thoughts, you will never see the light or the cleansing white cloud that washes away the old earth and makes your pure, to be able to see the Lord Most High. I have only seen just a speck of what is to come for all of us. There is so much more to look forward to. I feel blessed to have been able to get a hint of what the gates of heaven have in store for us. It is truly wonderful and exciting and it brings me peace.

And you and I will live forever.

Psalms 73:23-25 KJV

Nevertheless I am continually with thee:
You will hold my right hand.
You will guide me with your counsel, and
Afterwards you will receive me into glory.

Who do I have in heaven but you dear God.
And there is nothing here on earth but you that I desire.
My body and my heart might fail, but God is the strength of my
heart and my portion for ever.

Scriptures

I will say of the Lord. He is my refuge and my fortress: My God; in him will I trust. Psalm 91:2, KJV

Let not your heart be troubled: ye believe in God, believe also in me.

In my Father's house are many mansions: if it were not so, I would have told you. I go to prepare a place for you. And If I go and prepare a place for you, "I will come again and receive you unto myself; that where I am, there ye may be also. John 14:1-3, KJV

Λ

In the land beyond the Veil

I awoke one morning beyond the dawn to find my body bound. I felt God's hand upon my chest to say it was closing down.

The ambulance came and darkness took me off beyond their fold. A presence was standing by my side to keep away the cold.

She led me up into a land where darkness cannot be. Telling me to trust in her, and she would stand by me.

She sang in verse and melody that I would never die, that I would live forever in the rooms up in the sky.

She said that God was waiting with all the angels by his side, to welcome me in glory and where I will reside.

Passing with her through the cleansing veil I felt her nearness close. I saw the city far away where I would be with those.

Who had gone ahead of me and was standing at the gate, to welcome me with opened arms to come and join their wait.

Smiles and happiness came from all, with open arms unfurled, to bring me through the veil of life into their happy world.

I saw all my relatives, gone before, my parents, my siblings and friends. I saw Esther and Emma Ruth, my husband's mother and her kin.

I felt I had been here before in an earlier time of my life. I felt I had just returned from earth, where there was so much strife.

I felt happiness overwhelm my soul that gave out love to burst. I knew I still had a job to do so I must return to earth.

I went back to get my husband who would need my help for a while. Then we both would return to glory, to the land up in the sky.

And I was assured that we would return to this land beyond the veil, where we would reside forever, where God would reign as well.

Written by: Gladys L. Hargis & her

Angel,

Nov 26, 2010

The Heavens

I have a place to wander, beyond the space of time, with Jesus as my leader, to meet old friends of mine.

Where light never fails to be there, and my eyes can see so bright, the beauty of the heavenly realm, are caught up in my sight.

There is a place for all of us, to live eternally, to work, to play, to visit, and to worship every day.

Our leader is forever, not on the shelf of time. He has laid a plan for us, so we can be sublime.

We will see our parents every day, to join them at the throne, to worship our great leader, who will guide us in our home.

We have dropped our chains of earthly bonds, and feel free from toil and strife. Our loved ones will be there as well to enhance our life.

Heaven is a peaceful place to rest from earthly chores, a place to be so happy, with God and his angels galore.

A place where time will never end as promised by the Lord, I am glad to be a part of this and happy to be on board.

Written by: Gladys L. Hargis & her

Angel. Nov 28, 2010

About the Author

Warren and I were married in Holton Kansas, July 31, 1949.

I graduated from Hoyt, High School, Hoyt Kansas and continued my education in Business College. I was employed by the Santa Fe Railroad while Warren joined the Topeka Fire Department. I continued working until our son William was 5 months old. Then we took in day care children, finally foster children. We all helped build homes for our selves, and drove school buses part-time to help with our budget, so we could continue to help support all our children we had taken in to raise. We have one son William, 3 foster children, Joanie, Sandra, & Donnie. 8 foster grandchildren, 4 great grandchildren.

After we were empty nesters, we continued working for the State of Kansas, Warren as a Fire Officer, and I worked as a Driver for the Mentally Ill. We are now retired and living in Topeka, Kansas, with our cats Ollie and Bandit.

NOTES:

NOTES:

NOTES:

NOTES:

Notes:

NOTES:

NOTES:

NOTES:

Notes:

NOTES:

CPSIA information can be obtained at www.ICGtesting.com
Printed in the USA
LVOW092022120911

245951LV00010B/196/P